Nathanael Byfield

An account of the late revolution in New England

Nathanael Byfield

An account of the late revolution in New England

ISBN/EAN: 9783337235116

Printed in Europe, USA, Canada, Australia, Japan

Cover: Foto ©ninafisch / pixelio.de

More available books at **www.hansebooks.com**

AN

ACCOUNT

OF

The Late Revolution

IN

NEW-ENGLAND.

BY

Mr. NATHANAEL BYFIELD.

NEW YORK:
REPRINTED FOR JOSEPH SABIN.
1865.

AN

ACCOUNT

OF THE

𝕷ate 𝕽evolution

IN

NEW-ENGLAND.

Together with the

DECLARATION

OF THE

Gentlemen, Merchants, and Inhabitants of *BOSTON*,
and the Country Adjacent. *April* 18. 1689.

Written by Mr. *NATHANAEL BYFIELD*,
a Merchant of *Briſtol* in *New-England*, to his Friends
in *London*.

LICENSED, *June* 27. 1689.   *J. Fraſer.*

LONDON:
Printed for **Ric. Chiſwell**, at the *Roſe* and *Crown* in
St. *Paul's* Church-Yard.   MDCLXXXIX.

AN
ACCOUNT

OF THE

LATE REVOLUTION

IN

NEW-ENGLAND.

Written by M^r. *Nathanael Byfield*, to his Friends, *&c.*

GENTLEMEN,

ERE being an opportunity of fending for London, by a Veffel that loaded at Long-Ifland, and for want of a Wind put in here; and not knowing that there will be the like from this Country fuddenly, I am willing to give you fome brief Account of the moft remarkable Things that have

hapned here within this Fortnight laſt
paſt; concluding that till about that time,
you will have received *per Carter*, a full
Account of the management of Affairs
here. Upon the *Eighteenth* Inſtant, about
Eight of the Clock in the Morning, in
Boſton, it was reported at the South end
of the Town, That at the North end they
were all in Arms; and the like Report
was at the North end, reſpecting the South
end: Whereupon Captain *John George*
was immediately ſeized, and about Nine
of the Clock the Drums beat thorough the
Town; and an Enſign was ſet up upon
the Beacon. Then Mr. *Bradſtreet*, Mr.
Dantforth, Major *Richards*, Dr. *Cooke*, and
Mr. *Addington*, *&c.* were brought to the
Council-houſe by a Company of Soldiers
under the Command of Captain *Hill*.
The mean while the People in Arms, did
take up and put into Goal, Juſtice *Bulli-
vant*, Juſtice *Foxcroft*, Mr. *Randolf*, Sheriff
Sherlock, Captain *Ravenſcroft*, Captain
White, *Farewel*, *Broadbent*, *Crafford*, *Lar-
kin*, *Smith*, and many more, as alſo *Mercey*

the

the then Goal-keeper, and put *Scates* the Bricklayer in his place. About Noon, in the Gallery at the Council-houfe, was read the Declaration here inclofed. Then a Meffage was fent to the Fort to Sir *Edmund Androfs*, by Mr. *Oliver* and Mr. *Eyres*, figned by the Gentlemen then in the Council-Chamber, [which is here alfo inclofed]; to inform him how unfafe he was like to be if he did not deliver up himfelf, and Fort and Government forthwith, which he was loath to do. By this time, being about two of the Clock [the Lecture being put by] the Town was generally in Arms, and fo many of the Countrey came in, that there was twenty Companies in Bofton, befides a great many that appeared at Charles Town that could not get over [fome fay fifteen hundred]. There then came Information to the Soldiers, That a Boat was come from the Frigat that made towards the Fort, which made them hafte thither, and come to the Sconce foon after the Boat got thither; and 'tis faid that Governor *Androfs*, and

about

about half a score Gentlemen, were coming down out of the Fort; but the Boat being seized, wherein were small Arms, Hand-Granadoes, and a quantity of Match, the Governour and the rest went in again; whereupon Mr. *John Nelson*, who was at the head of the Soldiers, did demand the Fort and the Governor, who was loath to submit to them; but at length did come down, and was with the Gentlemen that were with him, conveyed to the Council-house, where Mr. *Bradstreet* and the rest of the Gentlemen waited to receive him; to whom Mr. *Stoughton* first spake, telling him, He might thank himself for the present Disaster that had befallen him, *&c.* He was then confined for that Night to Mr. *John Usher's* House under strong Guards, and the next Day conveyed to the Fort, [where he yet remains, and with him Lieutenant Collonel *Ledget*] which is under the Command of Mr. *John Nelson*; and at the Castle, which is under the Command of Mr. *John Fairweather*, is Mr. *West*, Mr. *Graham*, Mr. *Palmer*, and
Captain

Captain *Tryfroye*. At that time Mr. *Dudley* was out upon the Circuit, and was holding a Court at Southold on Long-Ifland. And on the 21ft Inftant he arrived at Newport, where he heard the News. The next Day Letters came to him, advifing him not to come home; he thereupon went over privately to Major *Smith's* at Naraganzett, and Advice is this Day come hither, that yefterday about a dozen young Men, moft of their own Heads, went thither to demand him; and are gone with him down to Bofton. We have alfo Advice, that on Fryday laft towards Evening, Sir *Edmond Androfs* did attempt to make an Efcape in Woman's Apparel, and pafs'd two Guards, and was ftopped at the third, being difcovered by his Shoes, not having changed them. We are here ready to blame you fometimes, that we have not to this Day received advice concerning the great Changes in England, and in particular how it is like to fair with us here; who do hope and believe that all thefe Things will work for

B our

our Good ; and that you will not be want-
ing to promote the Good of a Country
that ſtands in ſuch need as New England
does at this Day. The firſt Day of May,
according to former Uſage, is the Election
Day at Road Iſland ; and many do ſay
they intend their Choice there then. I
have not farther to trouble you with at
preſent, but recommending you, and all
our Affairs with you, to the Direction and
Bleſſing of our moſt Gracious God : I re-
main

        Gentlemen,
          Your moſt Humble
           Servant at Command,

           NATHANAEL BYFIELD.

Briſtol, *April* 29. 1689.

*Through the Goodneſs of God, there
  hath been no Blood ſhed.* Nath.
  Clark *is in* Plymouth *Gaol,
  and* John Smith *in* Gaol *here,
  all waiting for News from* England.

                             THE

THE

DECLARATION

OF THE

Gentlemen, Merchants and Inhabitants of *Boston*, and the Country Adjacent. *April* 18. 1689.

§ I. WE have seen more than a decad of Years rolled away since the English World had the Discovery of an horrid *Popish Plot* ; wherein the bloody Devotees of Rome had in their Design and Prospect no less than the Extinction of the *Protestant Religion :* which mighty Work they called *the utter subduing of a Pestilent Heresy* ; wherein [they said] there never were such Hopes of Success since the Death of Queen *Mary*, as now in our Days. And we were of all Men the most insensible, if we should apprehend a Countrey

trey fo remarkable for the true Profeffion
and pure Exercife of the Proteftant Religion as New-England is, wholly uncon-
cerned in the Infamous Plot. To crufh
and break a Countrey fo entirely and fig-
nally made up of *Reformed Churches*, and
at length to involve it in the miferies of
an utter Extirpation, muft needs carry
even a Supererogation of Merit with it
among fuch as were intoxicated with a
Bigotry infpired into them by the great
Scarlet Whore.

§ II. To get us within the reach of the
Defolation defired for us, it was no im-
proper thing that we fhould firft have our
Charter vacated, and the Hedge which
kept us from the wild Beafts of the Field,
effectually broken down. The Accom-
plifhment of this was haftned by the un-
wearied Sollicitations, and flanderous Ac-
cufations of a Man, for his *Malice* and
Falfhood, well known unto us all. Our
Charter was with a moft injurious Pretence
[and fcarce that] of Law, condemned before it was poffible for us to appear at
Weftminfter

Weftminfter in the legal Defence of it; and without a fair leave to anfwer for our felves, concerning the Crimes falfly laid to our Charge, we were put under a Prefident and Council, without any liberty for an Affembly, which the other American Plantations have, by a Commiffion from his Majefty.

§ III. The Commiffion was as *Illegal* for the Form of it, as the Way of obtaining it was *Malicious* and *Unreafonable:* yet we made no Refiftance thereunto as we could eafily have done; but chofe to give all Mankind a Demonftration of our being a People fufficiently dutiful and loyal to our King: and this with yet more Satisfaction, becaufe we took Pains to make our felves believe as much as ever we could of the Whedle then offer'd unto us; That his Magefty's Defire was no other than the happy Encreafe and Advance of thefe Provinces by their more immediate Dependance on the Crown of England. And we were convinced of it by the Courfes immediately taken to damp and fpoyl our Trade;

Trade; whereof Decayes and Complaints presently filled all the Country; while in the mean time neither the Honour nor the Treasure of the King was at all advanced by this new Model of our Affairs, but a considerable Charge added unto the Crown.

§ IV. In little more than half a Year we saw this Commission superseded by another yet more absolute and Arbitrary, with which Sir *Edmond Andros* arrived as our Governour: who besides his Power, with the Advice and Consent of his Council, to make Laws and raise Taxes as he pleased; had also Authority by himself to Muster and Imploy all Persons residing in the Territory as occasion shall serve; and to transfer such Forces to any English Plantation in America, as occasion shall require. And several Companies of Souldiers were now brought from Europe, to support what was to be imposed upon us, not without repeated Menaces that some hundreds more were intended for us.

§ V. The Government was no sooner in
these

thefe Hands, but Care was taken to load
Preferments principally upon fuch Men as
were Strangers to and Haters of the People:
and every ones Obfervation hath noted,
what Qualifications recommended a Man
to publick Offices and Employments, only
here and there a *good Man* was ufed, where
others could not eafily be had; the Governour himfelf, with Affertions now and
then falling from him, made us jealous that
it would be thought for his Majefties Intereft, if this People were removed and
another fucceeded in their room: And
his far-fetch'd Inftruments that were grow-
ing rich among us, would gravely inform
us, that it was not for his Majefties Intereft
that we fhould thrive. But of all our
Oppreffors we were chiefly *fqueez'd* by a
Crew of abject Perfons fetched from New
York, to be the Tools of the Adverfary,
ftanding at our right Hand; by thefe were
extraordinary and intollerable Fees extorted
from every one upon all Occafions, without any Rules but thofe of their own in-
fatiable Avarice and Beggary; and even
the

the probate of a Will muſt now coſt as
many *Pounds* perhaps as it did *Shilling*.
heretofore; nor could a ſmall Volume
contain the other Illegalities done by theſe
Horſe-leeches in the two or three Years
that they have been ſucking of us; and
what Laws they made it was as impoſſible
for us to know, as dangerous for us to
break; but we ſhall leave the Men of

*He would nei-
ther ſuffer them
to be printed
nor fairly pub-
liſhed.* Ipſwich or Plimotuh [among others] to
tell the Story of the Kindneſs which has
been ſhown them upon this Account
Doubtleſs a Land ſo ruled as once New-
England was, has not without many Fears
and Sighs beheld the wicked walking on
every Side, and the vileſt Men exalted.

§ VI. It was now plainly affirmed, both
by ſome in open Council, and by the ſame in
private Converſe, that the People in New-
England were all *Slaves*, and the only dif-
ference between them and *Slaves* is their
not being bought and ſold; and it was a
Maxim delivered in open Court unto us
by one of the Council, *that we muſt not
think the Priviledges of Engliſh men would
follow*

follow us to the End of the World: Accordingly we have been treated with multiplied Contradictions to *Magna Charta*, the Rights of which we laid claim unto. Persons who did but peaceably object against the raising of Taxes, without an Assembly, have been for it fined, some twenty, some thirty, and others fifty Pounds. Packt and pickt Juries have been very common things among us, when, under a pretended Form of Law, the Trouble of some honest and worthy Men has been aimed at: but when some of this Gang have been brought upon the Stage, for the most detestable Enormities that ever the Sun beheld, all Men have with Admiration seen what Methods have been taken that they might not be treated according to their Crimes. Without a Verdict, yea, without a Jury sometimes have People been fined most unrighteously; and some not of the meanest Quality have been kept in long and close Imprisonment without any the least Information appearing against them, or an *Habeas Corpus* allowed unto them. In

C   short,

fhort, when our Oppreffors have been a little out of Mony, 'twas but pretending fome Offence to be enquired into, and the moft innocent of Men were continually put into no fmall Expence to anfwer the Demands of the Officers, who muft have Mony of them, or a Prifon for them, tho none could accufe them of any Mifde-meanour.

§ VII. To plunge the poor People every where into deeper Incapacities, there was one very comprehenfive Abufe given to us; Multitudes of pious and fober Men through the Land, fcrupled the Mode of Swearing on the Book, defiring that they might Swear with an uplifted Hand, agreeable to the ancient Cuftom of the Colony; and though we think we can prove that the Common Law amongft us (as well as in fome other places under the Englifh Crown) not only indulges, but even commands and enjoins the Rite of lifting the Hand in *Swearing ;* yet they that had this Doubt, were ftill put by from ferving upon any Juries; and many of
them

them were moſt unaccountably Fined and Impriſoned. Thus one Grievance is a *Trojan Horſe*, in the Belly of which it is not eaſy to recount how many inſufferable Vexations have been contained.

§ VIII. Becauſe theſe Things could not make us miſerable faſt enough, there was a notable Diſcovery made of we know not what *flaw* in all our *Titles to our Lands;* and tho, *beſides* our purchaſe of them from the Natives ; and, *beſides* our actual peaceable unqueſtioned Poſſeſſion of them for near threeſcore Years, and beſides the Promiſe of K. *Charles* II. in his Proclamation ſent over to us in the Year 1683, That *no Man here ſhall receive any Prejudice in his Free-hold or Eſtate:* We had the Grant of our Lands, under the Seal of the Council of Plimouth: which Grant was Renewed and Confirmed unto us by King *Charles* I. under the Great Seal of England ; and the General Court which conſiſted of the Patentees and their Aſſociates, had made particular Grants hereof to the ſeveral *Towns* (though 'twas now deny'd by the

the Governour, that there was any fuch
Thing as a *Town*) among us; to all which
Grants the General Court annexed for the
further fecuring of them, *A General Act*,
publifhed under the Seal of the Colony,
in the Year 1684. Yet we were every
day told, *That no Man was owner of a Foot
of Land in all the Colony.* Accordingly,
Writs of Intrufion began every where to
be ferved on People, that after all their
Sweat and their Coft upon their formerly
purchafed Lands, thought themfelves *Free-
holders* of what they had. And the Governor caufed the Lands pertaining to thefe
and thofe *particular Men*, to be meafured
out for his Creatures to take poffeffion of;
and the *Right Owners*, for pulling up the
Stakes, have paffed through Moleftations
enough to tire all the Patience in the
World. They are more than a few, that
were by Terrors driven to take Patents
for their Lands at exceffive rates, to fave
them from the next that might petition
for them: and we fear that the forcing of
the People at the Eaftward hereunto, gave

too

too much Rife to the late unhappy Inva-
fion made by the Indians on them. Blanck
Patents were got ready for the reft of us,
to be fold at a Price, that all the Mony and
Moveables in the Territory could fcarce
have paid. And feveral Towns in the
Country had their Commons begg'd by
Perfons (even by fome of the Council
themfelves) who have been privately en-
couraged thereunto, by thofe that fought
for Occafions to impoverifh a Land already
Peeled, Meeted out and Trodden down.

§ IX. All the Council were not ingaged
in thefe ill Actions, but thofe of them
which were true Lovers *of their Country*,
were feldom admitted to, and feldomer
confulted at the Debates which produced
thefe unrighteous Things : Care was taken
to keep them under Difadvantages ; and
the Governor, with five or fix more, did
what they would. We bore all thefe, and
many more fuch Things, without making
any attempt for any Relief; only Mr.
Mather, purely out of refpect unto the
Good of his Afflicted Country, undertook

a Voyage into England; which when
these Men suspected him to be preparing
for, they used all manner of Craft and
Rage, not only to interrupt his *Voyage*,
but to ruin his *Person* too. God having
through many Difficulties given him to
arrive at White-hall, the King, more than
once or twice, promised him a certain
Magna Charta for a speedy Redress of
many Things which we were groaning
under: and in the mean time said, *That
our Governor should be written unto, to
forbear the Measures that he was upon.*
However, after this, we were injured in
those very Things which were complained
of; and besides what Wrong hath been
done in our Civil Concerns, we suppose
the Ministers and the Churches every where
have seen our Sacred Concerns apace go-
ing after them: How they have been
Discountenanced, has had a room in the
Reflection of every Man, that is not a
Stranger *in our Israel.*

§ X. And yet that our Calamity might
not be terminated here, we are again
Briar'd

Briar'd in the Perplexities of another Indian War ; how, or why, is a myſtery too
deep for us to unfold. And tho' 'tis
judged that our Indian Enemies are not
above 100. in Number, yet an Army of
One thouſand Engliſh hath been raiſed for
the Conquering of them ; which Army of
our poor Friends and Brethren now under
Popiſh Commanders (for in the Army as
well as in the Council, Papiſts are in
Commiſſion) has been under ſuch a Con-
duct, that not one Indian hath been kill'd,
but more Engliſh are ſuppoſed to have
died through ſickneſs and hardſhip, than
we have Adverſaries there alive ; and the
whole War hath been ſo managed, that
we cannot but ſuſpect in it, a Branch of
the Plot *to bring us low ;* which we leave
to be further enquir'd into in due time.

§ XI. We did nothing againſt theſe
Proceedings, but only cry to our God ;
they *have cauſed the cry of the Poor to come
unto him, and he hears the cry of the Afflicted.* We have been quiet hitherto, and ſo
ſtill we ſhould have been, had not the
Great

Great God at this time laid us under a double engagement to do fomething for our Security: befides, what we have in the ftrangely unanimous Inclination which our Countrymen by extreameft neceffities are driven unto. For firft, we are inform-ed that the reft of the Englifh America is alarmed with juft and great Fears, that they may be attaqu'd by the French, who have lately ('tis faid) already treated many of the Englifh with worfe then *Turkifh* Cruelties; and while we are in equal Danger of being furprifed by them, it is high time we fhould be better guarded, than we are like to be while the Govern-ment remains in the hands by which it hath been held of late. Moreover, we have underftood, (though the Governour has taken all imaginable care to keep us all ignorant thereof) that the Almighty God hath been pleafed to profper the noble Undertaking of the Prince of Orange, to preferve the three Kingdoms from the horrible brinks of Popery and Slavery, and to bring to a condign Punifhment thofe

worft

worſt of Men, by whom Engliſh Liberties
have been deſtroy'd; in compliance with
which glorious Action we ought ſurely to
follow the Patterns which the Nobility,
Gentry and Commonalty in ſeveral parts
of thoſe Kingdoms have ſet before us,
though *they* therein chiefly propoſed to
prevent what *we* already endure.

§ XII. We do therefore ſeize upon the
Perſons of thoſe few ill Men which have
been (next to our Sins) the grand Authors
of our Miſeries; reſolving to ſecure them,
for what Juſtice, Orders from his High-
neſs, with the Engliſh Parliament ſhall
direct, left, ere we are aware, we find
(what we may fear, being on all ſides in
Danger) our ſelves to be by them given
away to a Forreign Power, before ſuch
Orders can reach unto us; for which
Orders we now humbly wait. In the
mean time firmly believing, that we have
endeavoured nothing but what meer Duty
to God and our Country calls for at our
Hands: We commit our Enterpriſe unto
D   the

the Bleffing of Him, *who hears the cry of the Oppreffed*, and advife all our Neighbours, for whom we have thus ventured our felves, to joyn with us in Prayers and all juft Actions, for the Defence of the Land.

At the *Town-House* in *Boston, April* 18. 1689.

SIR,

OVR Selves and many others the Inhabitants of this Town, and the Places adjacent, being surprized with the Peoples sudden taking of Arms; in the first motion whereof we were wholly ignorant, being driven by the present Accident, are necessitated to acquaint your Excellency, that for the quieting and securing of the People inhabiting in this Country from the imminent Dangers they many ways lie open and exposed to, and tendring your own Safety, We judge it necessary you forthwith surrender and deliver up the Government and Fortification to be preserved and disposed according to Order and Direction from the Crown of England, which suddenly is expected may arrive; promising all security from violence to your Self or any of your Gentlemen or Souldiers in Person and Estate: Otherwise we are assured they will endeavour the taking of the Fortification by Storm, if any Opposition be made.

To Sir Edmond Andross *Kt.*

Waite Winthrop.	Elisha Cook.
Simon Bradstreet.	Isaac Addington.
William Stoughton.	John Nelson.
Samuel Shrimpton.	Adam Winthrop.
Bartholomew Gidney.	Peter Sergeant.
William Brown.	John Foster.
Thomas Danforth.	David Waterhouse.
John Richards.	

FINIS.